I love that you're my

# Stepdaughter

because

I Love You Because Books
www.riverbreezepress.com

# To my Stepdaughter

Love, _Jolie_

Date: _March 7, 2020_

# The best thing about you is your

Huge, caring and loving heart ♡

# Thank you for being patient with me when

We have to go to the vet and It takes fovever.

# I remember when we

Went to the market, bought the whole store, had way too much fun, and you found the skunk!

# You have a wonderful

Smile and laugh :)

# You make me feel special when

I get hugs and you let me snuggle you during story time.

# I am so proud of you for

How hard you work at everything you do.
& You should be *SO* proud of yourself.

# I love when you tell me about

Your days at school ♡

I love when we

*laugh & be silly*

together

# You taught me how to

To be confidant.

be a strong girl ! to be brave.

(⅓ Irish dance, but too bad I am HORRIBLE.)

# I know you love me because

I can feel it in my heart, and we have so much fun together.

# I wish I could

_dance, do art, sing, be creative/craft_

# as well as
# you do

# I love that we have the same

silly sense of humor
(sometimes dad thinks we
are nuts!)

# You should be the queen of

IRISH DANCE!

# You have an amazing talent for

Everything that you set your mind
to. (Especially Irish Dance and art!)

# You make me laugh when you

Dress up as Beatrice

(Dad has no clue!)

# I wish I had more time to

_Be silly /story time/ play_

## with you

You make the best

ART!

# You have
# inspired me to

be stronger, be more confidant, and
to be the best person and
step-Mom I can be.

# If I could give you anything it would be

A big house full of puppies and llamas.

# I would love to go

EVERYWHERE
_____

# with you!

# I am here for you
## whenever

you need me. I will always be here
for you, NO MATTER WHAT! ♡

# I love you
# because you are

So incredibly special to me.

Made in the USA
San Bernardino, CA
13 February 2020